Women in Politics and Government

BY AMANDA LANSER

CONTENT CONSULTANT
Heidi M. Berggren, PhD
Professor, Political Science and Women's and Gender Studies
University of Massachusetts Dartmouth

Essential Library

An Imprint of Abdo Publishing | abdopublishing.com

WOMEN'S LIVES in History

abdopublishing.com

Published by Abdo Publishing, a division of ABDO, PO Box 398166, Minneapolis, Minnesota 55439. Copyright © 2017 by Abdo Consulting Group, Inc. International copyrights reserved in all countries. No part of this book may be reproduced in any form without written permission from the publisher. Essential Library™ is a trademark and logo of Abdo Publishing.

Printed in the United States of America, North Mankato, Minnesota
052016
092016

THIS BOOK CONTAINS RECYCLED MATERIALS

Cover Photo: iStockphoto; Shutterstock Images
Interior Photos: Andrew Burton/Getty Images News/Thinkstock, 4–5, 90–91; George Grantham Bain Collection/Library of Congress, 7; Bain News Service/Library of Congress, 8–9, 12; Shutterstock Images, 13; AP Images, 14–15, 41, 42–43, 47; Murray Becker/AP Images, 17; Bettmann/Corbis, 18, 33, 35; Montgomery County Sheriff's Office/AP Images, 21; Themba Hadebe/AP Images, 23; Marci Stenberg/Merced Sun-Star/AP Images, 25; Rena Schild/Shutterstock Images, 27; John Lindsay/AP Images, 28–29; Charles Gorry/AP Images, 31; Sayyid Azim/AP Images, 37; John McConnico/AP Images, 39; Dan Kitwood/Getty Images News/Thinkstock, 44; Harry Cabluck/AP Images, 49; Charles Wenzelberg/AP Images, 51; Manuel Balce Ceneta/AP Images, 54–55; Martial Trezzini/Keystone/AP Images, 57; Evan Agostini/AP Images, 61; Doug Mills/AP Images, 62; Jessica Hill/AP Images, 64; Odd Andersen/AFP/Getty Images, 66–67; Sean Gallup/Getty Images News/Thinkstock, 69; Sergei Chuzavkov/AP Images, 71; Matt Rourke/AP Images, 73; Alex Wong/Getty Images News/Thinkstock, 76; Ethan Miller/Getty Images News/Thinkstock, 77; Jung Yeon-je/Pool Photo/AP Images, 78–79; Geoff Pugh/Rex Features/AP Images, 81; Jeff Roberson/AP Images, 85; John Bazemore/AP Images, 87; John Locher/AP Images, 89; Julia Reinhart/Demotix/Corbis, 94; Aya Batrawy/AP Images, 97

Editor: Mirella Miller
Series Designer: Maggie Villaume

Cataloging-in-Publication Data
Names: Lanser, Amanda, author.
Title: Women in politics and government / by Amanda Lanser.
Description: Minneapolis, MN : Abdo Publishing, [2017] | Series: Women's lives
  in history | Includes bibliographical references and index.
Identifiers: LCCN 2015960325 | ISBN 9781680782936 (lib. bdg.) |
  ISBN 9781680774870 (ebook)
Subjects: LCSH: Women--Juvenile literature. | Leadership in women--
  --Juvenile literature. | Women in the professions--Juvenile literature.
Classification: DDC 320--dc23
LC record available at http://lccn.loc.gov/2015960325

Contents

As a teenager, Malala received death threats but continued writing about her fear of the Taliban.

CHAPTER ONE

Breaking Ground

"Some people call me the girl who was shot by the Taliban. And some, the girl who fought for her rights," Malala Yousafzai told her audience at her Nobel Lecture.[1] The 17-year-old from Pakistan is the youngest person ever to receive a Nobel Peace Prize. Of 129 prize recipients, just 16 have been women.[2] After thanking her family and recognizing her corecipient, children's rights activist Kailash Satyarthi, Malala spoke articulately on the human right children have to receive an education.

An Islamist militant group called the Taliban controlled the community where Malala grew up. When she was 11, Malala began writing a blog describing her fear that Taliban soldiers would attack schools. Three years later, masked Taliban soldiers boarded Malala's school bus and shot her. While she recuperated from the attack at a hospital in the United Kingdom, the Pakistani people protested the Taliban in support of her. In a number of weeks, the Pakistani government responded to demands of the public and passed the Right to Free and Compulsory Education Act, guaranteeing free education for children up to 16 years old.

At the end of her Nobel Lecture, Malala stressed to her audience that girls—and boys—across the world continue to be denied an education every day. Her nonprofit organization, the Malala Fund, raises money for girls' education. "I had two options," she said. "One was to remain silent and wait to be killed. And the second was to speak up and then be killed. I chose the second one. I decided to speak up."[3]

Women around the World Fight for Suffrage

Malala is one voice in a long history of women around the world who have spoken up for the rights of women and girls, often in the face of violence. One of the most basic rights women have fought for is to participate in government as voters, legislators, judges, and political activists. Through the decades and in the face of incredible odds, women around the world have earned their way to the top levels of government, fought for their voices to be heard, and changed their communities and the world with their votes and their activism. These women were not perfect and did not always act perfectly, of course. But their words and actions made it possible for future women and girls to become politically active—and politically powerful.

The right to vote is known as suffrage. In the United States, the first organized effort for women's rights occurred in Seneca Falls, New York, in 1848. Many supporters of women's suffrage were also abolitionists fighting to end slavery and grant rights to former slaves. In 1869, suffrage movement leaders Elizabeth Cady Stanton and Susan B. Anthony formed the National Woman Suffrage Association. The group's primary goal was to pass a constitutional amendment giving women of all

In the United States and across the world, women have had to fight for the right to have their voices heard in government.

races the right to vote. Four years later, Anthony was arrested for voting in the 1872 presidential election. By the end of the decade, the woman suffrage amendment was debated in Congress but never passed.

While Stanton, Anthony, and countless other suffragists continued their work, states across the nation passed laws giving women the right to vote. Wyoming granted the vote to women in 1890. Over the next 30 years, 14 other states would follow Wyoming's example. The American public seemed ready to give women the vote. In fact, the people of Montana had already elected a female Congress member in 1916. Jeannette Rankin was the first female member of the US House of Representatives. In 1918, she introduced a bill that would create an amendment granting women the right to vote. It passed in the House and in the Senate one year later. In 1920,

STANTON AND ANTHONY

When Elizabeth Cady Stanton and Susan B. Anthony met in 1851, it is likely neither of them realized how significant their partnership would be for the rights of women in the United States and across the world. Stanton, an outspoken activist, and Anthony, an intrepid and inspiring leader, spent the next 41 years working together to gain the vote for women. They started the American Equal Rights Association and a newspaper called the *Revolution*. Its masthead declared, "Men their rights, and nothing more; women, their rights, and nothing less."[4] Stanton and Anthony both toured the country raising support for women's suffrage. Anthony also spoke in front of every Congress between 1869 and 1906 in support of a suffrage amendment. Both women died before the Nineteenth Amendment became law in 1920.

the Nineteenth Amendment was ratified by three-quarters of state legislatures and became the law of the land.[5]

YOUNG WOMEN MADE THE DIFFERENCE

Women of all ages, ethnicities, and backgrounds helped move women's rights in the United States forward. Jane Addams brought social services to poor, urban neighborhoods. She established Hull House, a place for herself and her workers to live, in Chicago, Illinois, in 1889. She was 29. A few years earlier, Nannie Helen Burroughs graduated from high school and immediately started teaching other African-American women job skills. At 31, she founded the National Training School for Women and Girls for African-American female students. Lucy Burns also put her education to work to support women's rights. She led the militant wing of US women's suffrage and founded the National Woman's Party in 1913 at age 34. That same year, 27-year-old Inez Milholland Boissevain became the symbol of woman's suffrage, appearing in marches in New York City and Washington, DC, in support of the vote.

Over the course of the 1900s, dozens of countries gave women the vote. Liechtenstein became the last nation in Europe to allow women to vote in 1984. South Africa did so for all women in 1994. Before that, only white women could vote. Bahrain, a country in the Middle East, granted women the vote in 2002. Saudi Arabia gave women the vote in 2015. Nearly 980 Saudi women ran for local office, and 20 of them won.[6] But not all countries have done so. Three countries—Brunei, the United Arab Emirates, and Lebanon—have broad restrictions on voting. Brunei and the United Arab Emirates are monarchies. They limit voting for both men and women. Lebanon allows women over 21 years old to vote only if they have an elementary education.

Women in Government Create Change

Today, women in the United States and countries across the globe serve as presidents, prime ministers, judges, and members of legislatures. Others use their platforms as First Ladies, attorneys, and political activists to speak out on local and world issues. Decades of work have brought social, economic, and political change in places where women are active in government, from Jeannette Rankin introducing an amendment to grant women the right to vote to Malala Yousafzai standing up for a girl's right to an education.

ALL WOMEN, NOT JUST WHITE WOMEN

The women's rights movement in the United States in the late 1800s and early 1900s included women of color. After the American Civil War (1861–1865), Congress passed the Fifteenth Amendment in 1870 guaranteeing the rights of African-American men to vote. African-American women still could not vote. This upset women's suffrage activists. Stanton and Anthony opposed the terms of the Fifteenth Amendment, believing it to be an extension of the oppression of rights for women. Over the next 50 years, women of all ethnicities worked to win the vote for women, but not always together. While some African-American women joined existing women's rights organizations that white women had established, others formed their own groups, such as the Alpha Suffrage Club. In the early 1900s, some African-American women faced discrimination within the women's rights movement. Despite these tensions, women of all ethnicities were granted the right to vote when the Nineteenth Amendment passed in 1920. But it would take another 45 years and the passage of the Voting Rights Act of 1965 for African-American women and men to fully exercise their right to vote.

Female Nobel Peace Prize
Winners

Of the 129 Nobel Peace Prizes awarded since 1901, just 16 have been awarded to women. The Nobel Peace Prize is awarded to people who work to bring peace between nations, reduce standing armies, and facilitate peace talks.[7]

1905
Baroness Bertha von Suttner, Austrian, peace activist and author of the antiwar novel *Lay Down Your Arms!*

1931
Jane Addams, American, founder of the Women's International League for Peace and Freedom (WILPF)

1946
Emily Greene Balch, American, work for reducing standing armies and peace and leader of WILPF

1976
Mairead Corrigan, Irish, cofounder of Community of Peace People; Betty Williams, Irish, cofounder of Community of Peace People

1979
Mother Teresa, Albanian/Indian, humanitarian worker in India and founder of Missionaries of Charity

1982

Alva Myrdal, Swedish, work toward nuclear disarmament

1991

Aung San Suu Kyi, Burmese, cofounder of the National League for Democracy in Burma

1992

Rigoberta Menchú Tum, Guatemalan, work for reconciliation between ethnic groups

1997

Jody Williams, American, founder of the International Campaign to Ban Landmines

2003

Shirin Ebadi, Iranian, work for democracy and the rights of women and children

2004

Wangari Maathai, Kenyan, founder of the Green Belt Movement fighting deforestation

2011

Leymah Gbowee, Liberian, work toward peace and women's rights and safety

Tawakkol Karman, Yemeni, work toward peace and women's rights and safety; Ellen Johnson Sirleaf, Liberian, work toward peace and women's rights and safety

2014

Malala Yousafzai, Pakistani, work for the right of all children to receive an education

Women had the opportunity to work outside the home in factories during World War II.

CHAPTER TWO

Setting the Stage for Change

During World War II (1939–1945), women assembled ammunition and aircraft, decoded secret messages, and served in the military as nurses. The US government provided funding for childcare for working mothers through 1946. But after the war, returning servicemen replaced many women who had worked full time. For many women, the desire to work did not go away, nor did the need for income. In the 1950s and 1960s, women across the world participated in the effort to define human rights worldwide and civil rights in the United States and South Africa.

Roosevelt Drafts a Bill of Human Rights

Eleanor Roosevelt was no stranger to politics when President Harry S. Truman appointed her to the United Nations (UN) Commission on Human Rights in

1946. As a young woman, Roosevelt had been a social worker, and she had been a volunteer for the American Red Cross during World War I (1914–1918). After the war, she became involved in the League of Women Voters and Women's Trade Union League. She served as First Lady during President Franklin D. Roosevelt's administration in the 1930s and 1940s.

Roosevelt was the only woman on the drafting committee for the UN Human Rights Commission, and she served as its first chairperson. Over three sessions in 1947 and 1948, she and her fellow delegates drafted the Universal Declaration of Human Rights (UDHR). The document's 30 articles outlined the basic human rights of people across the globe. The articles declare all humans have the right to freedom of life, liberty, and security and freedom from torture, inhumane treatment, slavery, and exile. The UN adopted the UDHR on December 10, 1948.

Roosevelt's political career did not end at the Human Rights Commission. In 1961, President John F. Kennedy appointed Roosevelt chair of the Presidential Commission on the Status of Women. The group studied the status of women's equality in the workplace, in the classroom, and in law. The commission found rampant discrimination against women in matters of wages and work hours, legal representation, and insurance and tax laws. The report recommended the federal government establish paid maternity leave, equal-opportunity hiring processes, and affordable childcare. The report provided direction for the growing number of US women dissatisfied with the status quo.

Because of her background, Roosevelt had credibility
with political leaders the world over when working
on the UN Human Rights Commission.

Eleanor Roosevelt

(1884–1962)

A nna Eleanor Roosevelt was born in 1884 in New York City. The niece of President Theodore Roosevelt, Eleanor was primarily raised by her grandmother after the deaths of her parents in the 1890s. Though her grandmother was a cold, verbally abusive woman, she provided Eleanor with an excellent education.

Roosevelt put her education to work for social justice in New York City. She put her work on hold to raise her family and support her husband's political career, becoming his political advocate and ally after he was struck with polio. Her political work through the 1920s and 1930s focused on voting and worker rights and continued after she became First Lady in 1933. Eleanor was well liked in the United States and abroad, a reputation that served her well after World War II in her work on human rights and other humanitarian causes.

Friedan Unveils *The Feminine Mystique*

One of those dissatisfied women was Betty Friedan. The Smith College graduate was a housewife living in New York when her alma mater asked her to conduct a survey for her 15-year reunion.

At the time of Friedan's survey, men were breadwinners, whereas women were expected to feel fulfilled in their roles as wives and mothers. The survey found many Smith alumnae were dissatisfied with their roles as housewives. Friedan later defined this as "the problem that has no name."[1] Society encouraged women to lose their sense of identity when they became wives and mothers. They were urged to focus exclusively on the needs of their families. Friedan argued that society taught women to blame themselves if they did not find satisfaction and fulfillment in their housework. She published her findings in a book in 1963. *The Feminine Mystique* was an immediate success that found support with white, educated, middle-class readers who, similar to the Smith alumnae, felt dissatisfied in their roles as wives and mothers.

Inspired by the success of her book, Friedan founded the National Organization for Women (NOW) in 1966. In its first ten years, NOW took action to change a wide variety of federal laws the group believed discriminated against women. It drafted a bill of rights

SECOND-WAVE FEMINISM

The first paperback edition of Friedan's book *The Feminine Mystique* sold 1.4 million copies.[2] The book was the catalyst for a movement called second-wave feminism. The first wave of feminism occurred during the US suffrage movement in the late 1800s and early 1900s. Though *The Feminine Mystique* largely ignored the plight of working-class women and women of color, the second wave of feminism it inspired drew these women to the cause. Activists pushed for the right to participate in politics and the workforce and worked to banish legal discrimination based on gender or ethnicity.

for women that called for the passage of the Equal Rights Amendment (ERA) and publicly funded childcare. NOW also called for the repeal of laws prohibiting abortion, and laws banning gender discrimination in hiring and firing. The group held numerous public protests and lobbied Congress for changes to federal law.

EQUAL RIGHTS AMENDMENT

In 1923, US suffragist Alice Paul introduced the ERA to Congress. It took 49 years of dedicated hard work on behalf of women's rights advocates to get the amendment passed in 1972. Though passed by Congress, the ERA was not ratified by the states—it was three states short of the necessary votes, so it did not become part of the Constitution. The text of the ERA is simple. The first section states, "Equality of rights under the law shall not be denied or abridged by the United States or by any state on account of sex."[3]

Parks Stands Up to Racism

While Roosevelt and Friedan worked for human rights and women's rights, another woman was challenging the status quo on civil rights. On December 1, 1955, Rosa Parks boarded a city bus in Montgomery, Alabama. She passed the first ten rows of seats to find a place toward the back, where city law required African Americans to sit. The law also required African Americans to give up their seat if a white rider could not find a seat.

Soon, the driver of Parks's bus asked her to give up her seat. Parks politely but firmly refused. The driver called the police, who arrested Parks. Her conviction inspired a citywide boycott of the Montgomery bus system. The boycott had a devastating effect on the city's economy, as African Americans accounted for 75 percent of all bus riders in the city.[4] Meanwhile, the US Supreme Court upheld a ruling that segregation on public buses was unconstitutional. Montgomery then reversed its policy of racial segregation on its city buses.

Though spontaneous, Parks's refusal to give up her seat was not surprising. She was an active member of the National Association for the Advancement of Colored People (NAACP). Though her protest made the news, Parks was not asked to comment on it as other male civil rights leaders were. Despite this, her protest inspired women of all ethnicities and classes to find their political voices.

Mandela Faces Down Apartheid

A few years after Parks's protest, young social worker Winnie Madikizela attended a meeting of the African National

The boycott that started after Parks's arrest lasted more than a year.

Congress (ANC), a black nationalist political party in South Africa. Her work at a Johannesburg hospital had inspired Madikizela to get involved in South African politics. At the ANC meeting, Madikizela met fellow civil rights worker Nelson Mandela, whom she would marry in 1958. Both Mandelas were active in the fight for rights for black citizens of South Africa. Racial segregation was legal and widespread in South Africa, where a white minority held political and economic power over a black majority. Starting in 1948, a number of federal laws systematized this racial segregation in a policy that became known as apartheid.

In 1960, the white South African government banned the ANC from political activity. The group took its activities underground, conducting acts of sabotage against the South African government.

APARTHEID

The legal, systematic policy of segregation and discrimination of the black majority in South Africa is called apartheid. Under apartheid, black South Africans were not allowed to serve in government. They were prohibited from owning property on 80 percent of South Africa's land.[5] When white and black South Africans did share space, as they did in urban areas, facilities such as bathrooms were separated by race. Activists, including Winnie Mandela, protested the unjust policies under apartheid and worked to end it. Some of these protests turned violent at the hands of the South African government, drawing the ire of other nations. South Africa relaxed its apartheid policies throughout the 1980s and abolished them entirely in 1994.

Winnie Mandela had been formally banned from the South African government when her husband was jailed. She was prohibited from associating with other civil rights activists, giving speeches, or even leaving her home or village. But despite these restrictions, she printed and distributed pamphlets on behalf of the ANC.

Mandela was a popular figure with many black South Africans.

Though the government had tried to suppress Mandela's political activism, her banishment seemed to make her belief in her cause stronger and more militant. Her confinement continued through the 1960s and 1970s, but she continued to work for the rights of black South Africans. After an uprising of black youths in 1976, Mandela founded the Black Women's Federation and the Black Parents' Association.

Her work continued through the 1980s and 1990s, during which time her actions and words became more controversial. She called for the killing of her opponents in a 1986 speech and was convicted of the kidnapping of alleged police informant Stompie Seipei. In 1994, the policy of apartheid finally ended in South Africa. Mandela was elected to parliament, while her husband became the first black president of South Africa. During her tenure, Mandela became president of the ANC's Women's League, where she helped advance women's rights in South Africa. Though a controversial figure, Mandela dedicated her life to fighting apartheid and systemic racism in South Africa.

Huerta Fights for Farmworkers

Like Mandela, Dolores Huerta was no stranger to systemic discrimination. Huerta fought to secure the basic rights of California's farmworkers. As a teacher, she was unhappy seeing her students come to school hungry and without adequate clothing. She believed the best way to help them was to give their farmworker parents more political power. She joined and became a leader of the Stockton Community Service Organization (CSO) in the 1950s and also founded the Agricultural Workers Association, which helped register farmworkers to vote.

At a CSO meeting in 1962, Huerta met fellow activist Cesar Chavez. The two activists wanted to organize farmworkers into unions, work that was beyond the scope of the CSO. That same year, they

Huerta, *left*, worked on behalf of
California farmworkers into the 2000s.

founded the National Farm Workers Association. In 1965, Huerta's group led a strike against California grape growers to protest their labor policies. Approximately 5,000 grape workers protested, along with consumers who boycotted California-grown grapes.[6] The boycott worked. In a few months, Huerta's group had convinced the grape growers to change their policies.

In 1967, the National Farm Workers Association merged with the Agricultural Workers Association to become the United Farm Workers Organizing Committee. It lobbied the California state government to provide disability insurance and state aid for farmworkers. The organization lobbied for the Agricultural Labor Relations Act of 1975, which gave farmworkers the right to unionize and negotiate better working conditions and wages.

GANDHI BECOMES PRIME MINISTER

Indira Gandhi was India's first female prime minister. She served three terms in the 1960s and 1970s and a fourth between 1980 and 1984, when she was assassinated. Gandhi's father had been the first prime minister of India. Gandhi joined her father's administration in 1955. She became a minister in her father's successor's administration, and upon his death became prime minister. As prime minister, in 1971 she led India in a victory against Pakistan to create the independent country of Bangladesh. She faced political opposition in 1975 and was convicted of violating election rules. While she appealed the court decision, Gandhi declared special emergency rule and passed several controversial laws that restricted personal freedoms. After two years, she was ousted and spent a brief time in prison, managing to be elected to parliament on her release. She rose through the ranks and became prime minister once again in 1980. Her fourth administration was wrought with political opposition that frequently became violent. Gandhi was assassinated by two of her own bodyguards.

Huerta received the Presidential Medal of
Freedom from President Barack Obama in 2012.

Civil and human rights at home and abroad were the primary focus of many female political

figures in the 1950s. Their work helped pave the way for women in the 1960s to demand more

political, economic, and social opportunities.

As prime minister, Meir's primary goal was to maintain peace for Israel—even if that meant the nation going to war to defend itself.

CHAPTER THREE

Making Waves in Court and Congress

The 1970s was a decade of rapid change in the political landscape for women in the United States and across the globe. Women became legislators, judges, and heads of state. Many continued fighting for the rights of women, the poor, and the environment. But as the movement of second-wave feminism against legal and widespread gender discrimination became more popular, some women spoke out against the sweeping social and political changes some activists demanded.

Meir Becomes Prime Minister

When she took office in 1969, Golda Meir became the first female prime minister of Israel. The country had formed only 21 years before, after the end of World War II. Meir was born in Russia but raised in the United States. She and her family were Jewish and had faced discrimination in Russia. While growing up in Milwaukee, Wisconsin, Meir became an activist against the violence Jews endured in Russia and the new oppressive Communist republic of Ukraine.

Drawn to the Holy Land, Meir moved to the Middle East in 1921. She remained active in politics through the end of World War II and became one of 25 signers of Israel's declaration of independence. She served as the new country's minister to the Soviet Union for a year before being elected to the Israeli parliament in 1949. In 1969, her political party elected her as its candidate for prime minister. Her term as prime minister was defined by her diplomacy regarding Israel's relationship with its Arab neighbors. In October 1973, this relationship reached a breaking point. Egypt and Syria attacked Israel on the Jewish holy day of Yom Kippur, starting a monthlong war that nearly ended in defeat for Israel. The conflict ended without a clear victor. Israel's lack of readiness was a surprise for many Israelis, eventually costing Meir her post. She resigned as prime minister in April 1974.

Chisholm Goes to Washington

The same year Meir was named prime minister of Israel, Shirley Chisholm became the first female African American elected to US Congress. She served seven consecutive terms between 1969 and 1983, during which time she advocated for the rights of women and children and against the Vietnam War (1955–1975). She helped found the Congressional Black Caucus, the Congressional Women's Caucus, and the National Political Congress of Black Women. She even ran for president.

"Ladies and Gentlemen . . . this is Fighting Shirley Chisholm coming through!" was Chisholm's congressional campaign cry in her home district in Brooklyn, New York.[1] Chisholm had already been a member of the New York state legislature for five years. Once elected, Chisholm focused her efforts on legislation that would benefit the lives of working men and women, especially those of color. She fought to extend day-care hours, create a mandatory minimum income, and provide more federal funds for education.

In 1972, Chisholm decided to run for president. She felt none of her fellow candidates represented the interests of African Americans or the inner-city poor. Women, welfare recipients, Hispanics, and white liberals supported Chisholm's campaign, but she found opposition in an unlikely place: the Congressional Black

The outspoken Chisholm ran her congressional campaign from the ground, connecting with the people who would vote her into office.

Caucus. The men of the caucus were upset that Chisholm had not consulted them before launching her campaign. Though her run was not successful, it did bring national attention to Chisholm's work and cause.

Steinem Speaks Up for Women's Rights

Similar to Betty Friedan, women's rights activist and writer Gloria Steinem was a Smith College alumna. Though the two women worked together for women's rights, Friedan and Steinem did not always get along. Steinem built on the ideas Friedan wrote about in *The Feminine Mystique* to include the freedom to have sexual relations outside of marriage, which Friedan did not focus on. Despite their differences, Friedan and Steinem teamed up to cofound the National Women's Political Caucus in 1971. Chisholm was also a founding member. The group finds, trains, and supports women who want to run for political office. In 1971, women held just 1 percent of US political offices.[2] The caucus had a nearly immediate effect on the number of women in political office. In 1972, 28 percent more women held state legislative seats.[3] In 2015, women held 19.4 percent of US congressional seats and 24.4 percent of state legislative seats.[4]

CONGRESSIONAL BLACK CAUCUS

Thirteen African-American members of Congress founded the Congressional Black Caucus (CBC) in 1971.[5] The group works on behalf of the underrepresented US citizens, such as the poor and people of color. The CBC works to expand access to higher education and fair compensation, reduce differences in health care between social and ethnic groups, and create foreign policy that aligns with the UN Declaration of Human Rights. The group pushed for making Martin Luther King Jr.'s birthday a national holiday. It was the first—and only—time a person of color was honored with a national holiday.

Steinem's *Ms.* magazine
discussed issues from a
feminist perspective.

TITLE IX

In 1972, Congress passed landmark legislation called Title IX. It bans discrimination based on gender for any educational program or activity that receives federal funds. Primary schools, secondary schools, universities, and other educational organizations that receive federal funds must follow Title IX laws. When Title IX went into effect, it opened dozens of male-only universities and colleges to women and gave girls the chance to play sports in school and win athletic scholarships. It made sexual harassment at a place of learning illegal, and it educated women and men about how to spot and prevent it. Women and girls now had the right to study science and math, become doctors or engineers, or enter other professions previously reserved for men. Counselors could no longer pressure female students into traditionally female coursework and careers.

In 1972, Steinem started *Ms.* magazine. *Ms.* was often provocative. Its first issue featured famous women who had had abortions, a hot topic in the early 1970s and today.

Steinem was a supporter of the ERA, advocating for the amendment before the US Senate in 1970. She argued opposition to the ERA stemmed from myths about the differences between the genders that benefited men and oppressed women. She faced stiff opposition from conservative activist Phyllis Schlafly, who had become a leader of a grassroots movement against second-wave feminism. In the years following, Steinem's activism led to the creation of several organizations and the first national day for girls: Take Our Daughters to Work Day.

Schlafly Speaks for Conservative Women

An attorney and mother of six children, Phyllis Schlafly and her supporters believed the women's rights agenda posed a threat to American families. Schlafly's grassroots pro-family movement focused

Sarah Weddington

Sarah Weddington was 26 years old when she argued in front of the Supreme Court of the United States. The Texas attorney represented a client who was challenging the state of Texas's antiabortion laws, and by 1972, their case had been appealed all the way to the Supreme Court.

Weddington made a strong case against Texas's antiabortion laws. In 1973, the Supreme Court issued its ruling. In a 7–2 decision, the justices ruled that Texas—and therefore the other 49 states—could no longer outlaw abortions.[6] The ruling, known as *Roe v. Wade*, became a hot-button issue immediately. Women's rights activists applauded the decision, while conservative activists immediately set to work to overturn it.

Winning such a case would make any attorney's career. But Weddington was still in her twenties. She served in the Texas House of Representatives beginning in 1973, during which time she fought for women's rights, worked to reform state laws governing rape, and tried to block laws limiting abortions. In 1978, she became chair of President Jimmy Carter's administration's Interdepartmental Task Force on Women, which worked to appoint more women to government posts. Weddington continued to serve in the Carter administration until January 1981.

(1945–)

on defeating the passage of the ERA. Her organization Stop Taking Our Privileges (STOP) argued that the ERA took away important privileges American women enjoyed, including exemption from the national draft and some social security benefits. STOP argued the ERA would hurt women and their families, not help them.

Schlafly found support from more conservative women across the country. In her outspoken opposition, Schlafly found herself arguing with Steinem and other women's rights activists. Schlafly and STOP were ultimately successful in the battle against the ERA. Though Congress passed it in 1972, it did not get the necessary support of 38 states to become ratified.[7] Schlafly and STOP had awakened a large bloc of conservative voters and made Schlafly into a conservative powerhouse. She worked on several Republican campaigns and became a delegate to the Republican National Convention. Schlafly and STOP's work reached out to motivate conservatives to vote. Their work would help elect Republican presidential candidate Ronald Reagan to office in 1980.

Maathai Starts a Movement

While American women debated the merits of the ERA, Wangari Maathai made strides for rural African women. She was the first woman in east and central Africa to earn a doctorate degree and became the first female professor in her home country of Kenya. She saw firsthand how poor land management affected rural, poor women and their families. When forests were cut down to make room for agriculture, women had to travel farther for firewood. Water sources became scarcer, and growing and finding food became more difficult. When women spent more time and resources on finding ways to survive, they became disempowered and disenfranchised.

In 1977, Maathai started a grassroots movement to stop deforestation. The Green Belt Movement encouraged rural women to plant trees and consider the environment before making changes to their properties. Maathai's movement planted 30 million trees in Kenya.[8] Managed correctly, trees give soil more structure and provide firewood. Maathai also helped women store rainwater to reduce water scarcity and ran workshops to help women become active in local politics.

Maathai continued her work into the 1980s and 1990s. By the 2000s, she had become a member of the Parliament of Kenya. She received the Nobel Peace Prize in 2004 for her work. She was the first African woman to receive the prize.

Maathai plants a tree in Nairobi as part of the Green Belt Movement.

Ebadi Stands for Justice

As Maathai worked to expand women's rights in Kenya, Shirin Ebadi experienced a dramatic reversal of women's rights in Iran. Ebadi became one of Iran's first female judges in 1969 and the first female chief justice of the city court of Tehran in 1975. But in February 1979, she and Iran's other female judges were abruptly dismissed from their positions.

A month before, powerful Shiite Muslim cleric Ayatollah Ruhollah Khomeini had overthrown the shah, who had been Iran's ruler for four decades. Within two weeks, Khomeini had replaced the shah's nonreligious government with a theocracy run by powerful Muslim leaders. The new government repealed many women's rights. They were replaced with sharia law, which required Iranians to follow Islamic laws of how to dress and behave.

Though an experienced attorney and justice, Ebadi was made a clerk in the court over which she had once presided. She protested and became a consultant within the Justice Department, but this demotion was too much to bear. By 1992, Ebadi had asked for early retirement so she could start her own law practice. She went on to represent women, children, and others who had lost rights in the Islamic Revolution. Ebadi also founded several organizations dedicated to human rights, including

Ebadi, *right*, receives the Nobel Peace Prize in Oslo, Norway.

the Human Rights Defence Centre. In 2003, Ebadi won the Nobel Peace Prize for her work to secure the human rights of women and children. She was only the fifth Muslim to win the prize and the first Muslim woman to do so.[11]

The 1970s brought many political, economic, and social changes for women in the United States and around the world. But not all these changes were popular with all women. What some saw as basic rights, others perceived as destroying cultural norms and traditions. The decade ended with more women elected to political office and legal discrimination repealed. But there was still much work to be done.

1979
Islamic Revolution

The Islamic Revolution set back much of Iranian women's rights overnight. It would take decades more work for women to gain back the modest rights they had won before 1979.

BEFORE THE 1979 ISLAMIC REVOLUTION
Women could serve in government.
Women could petition for divorce and custody of their children.
Wives were free to work.

AFTER THE 1979
ISLAMIC REVOLUTION

Women were removed from most government posts.

Divorce and custody rights were repealed; men had automatic custody of their children and could take up to four wives.

Husbands could stop their wives from traveling (including to go vote) and working.

Women in Iran quickly lost their rights during the Islamic Revolution.

Thatcher was the longest continually serving prime minister of the United Kingdom since 1827.

UNITED

CHAPTER FOUR

Women Rising

W omen across the world made great strides in politics in the 1960s and 1970s. In the 1980s, women achieved new heights in government office and political activism. Though many still found themselves to be the only woman in the room, female leaders in government and politics were becoming more common.

Thatcher Earns the Nickname Iron Lady

When Margaret Thatcher became the United Kingdom's first female prime minister in 1979, she had already spent 20 years battling her Labour Party opponents in Parliament. A member and leader of the Conservative Party, Thatcher was an outspoken critic of policies she felt threatened the strength of the British economy. Her approach to governing became known as Thatcherism, characterized by strong love of country, unwavering support for what she thought was right, and uncompromising dedication to her goals.

In her first term, Thatcher focused on reversing the economic decline of the 1970s. She lowered some taxes and raised others while privatizing many state-owned businesses and utilities. Despite these efforts, the country still

Thatcher was firm in her diplomacy with the crumbling Soviet Union, earning her the nickname Iron Lady.

experienced high unemployment and inflation, and public opinion of Thatcher was low. Then, the military-led government of Argentina invaded the Falkland Islands, British territory off the eastern coast of Argentina. Thatcher took a firm stand against the invasion, taking military action when diplomacy failed. Her reaction to the conflict won her popularity among Britons and helped her party keep its majority in Parliament with her as prime minister.

In her second and third terms, Thatcher continued her conservative reforms of the British government and economy. In 1984, she survived an assassination attempt by the Irish Republican Army (IRA), an organization she and others considered a terrorist group. The IRA demanded a republic for Northern Ireland, a territory of the United Kingdom. Though she took a firm stand against the independent IRA, she encouraged cooperation between the British and Irish governments, both of which wanted control over Northern Ireland. At home, Thatcher passed a national education curriculum, introduced competition between health-care providers in the National Health Service, and enacted a controversial new tax system for local governments.

But one policy would lead to Thatcher's political decline. She diverged from her party's view about how integrated the United Kingdom should become with the rest of Europe. The Conservative Party, including most of Thatcher's advisers, was traditionally pro-Europe, but Thatcher resisted further

THE IRA

When Thatcher became prime minister of the United Kingdom, she inherited tension between the British government and Northern Ireland. Supporters of Northern Ireland, a British territory, wanted the region to reunify with Ireland. The conflict caused decades of military and political strife starting at the turn of the 1900s. The IRA was created in 1919 as the unofficial military of Northern Ireland. The group clashed with British prime ministers for decades. The peak of the violence occurred between 1969 and 1994, a period known as the Long War. It was during this time that the IRA attempted to assassinate Thatcher. In 1994, the IRA began the slow process of disarming itself and instead using diplomacy, not military force, to fight its battles, a policy it continues today.

integration with the rest of the continent. Her advisers withdrew their support, and Thatcher was forced to resign in 1990.

Mankiller Leads an Indigenous Nation

While Thatcher was making history in the United Kingdom, Wilma Mankiller was making history in the Cherokee Nation in North America. In 1985, she became the first female principal chief of the Cherokee Nation. During that time, the tribe's membership more than doubled while its economy expanded to provide job training, health care, and better education for toddlers and school-age children.

Born on her family's land in Oklahoma, Mankiller and her family were relocated to San Francisco, California, by the US Bureau of Indian Affairs in the hope that moving to a city would increase employment among American Indians. Mankiller later described the move as "my own little Trail of Tears."[1] The Trail of Tears was the forced relocation of 15,000 members of the Cherokee Nation from their land in Georgia, North Carolina, Tennessee, Alabama, Missouri, Illinois, and Arkansas to Oklahoma in the early 1800s.[2] More than a quarter of those who were forced to relocate did not survive the march.[3]

While in San Francisco, Mankiller married and had children. But similar to Friedan, she was not satisfied with housework and raising her kids. She wanted to become more involved in politics, especially American Indian activism. She helped shuttle supplies to native protesters who occupied Alcatraz Island between 1969 and 1971. Eventually, Mankiller returned to Oklahoma.

Mankiller and her family returned to Oklahoma in 1977 to get involved in the tribal government.

Mankiller became the economic stimulus coordinator for the Cherokee Nation and volunteered in other aspects of tribal government. In 1981, she founded a new government department dedicated to improving housing and community resources. Principal Chief Ross Swimmer noticed Mankiller's hard work and asked her to be his running mate in the 1983 election. Swimmer won reelection and Mankiller became the first female deputy chief of the Cherokee Nation. Two years later, Swimmer resigned to pursue a job in the US federal government, making Mankiller the Cherokee Nation's first female principal chief.

As principal chief, Mankiller focused on increasing tribal membership, expanding the tribe's annual budget, and providing more services to members. She funded job-training programs and improved tribal health care. Mankiller also expanded support for the tribe's education system, building a high school in Oklahoma and expanding the tribe's preschool program. Mankiller was a popular chief, winning reelection with more than 80 percent of the vote.[4] But she was forced to resign in 1995 after years of poor health. She continued to advise other tribal politicians and remain active in government until her death in 2010.

O'Connor Takes a Seat on the Supreme Court

When she was appointed as the first female justice of the United States Supreme Court, Sandra Day O'Connor was used to being one of the only women in the room. She was one of three women in her graduating class at Stanford Law School in 1952.[5] She ranked third in her class behind future Chief Justice William Rehnquist.[6] As a young attorney in California, O'Connor discovered many law firms would not hire her because she was a woman. Undaunted, she became an attorney for the city of San Mateo, California, for one year.

O'Connor continued to practice law while raising her three sons. Conservative-leaning O'Connor also became more active in politics. In 1965, she took a position as an assistant attorney general in Arizona, and a year later she was appointed to replace her state senator. O'Connor served in the state senate for five years and became the first woman in the nation to become a majority leader in a state senate.

After her time in the state senate, O'Connor became a county judge and by the late 1970s had become a judge in the Arizona Court of Appeals. In July 1981, President Reagan nominated O'Connor to

O'Connor's background set her up to successfully serve on the US Supreme Court.

become the first woman to serve as a Supreme Court justice.

When she joined the bench, O'Connor became the first justice in 24 years to have state court experience and the first in 32 years who had served as a legislator. With an understanding of how law and lawmaking worked on the state level, O'Connor took a measured approach to her role as justice. She did not support much of the platform of the women's movement and had a mixed judicial record on abortion. She had, however, fought gender discrimination in the Arizona bar exam and founded two professional associations for female attorneys and judges. As a justice, she did not rule in a way Republicans or Democrats could predict.

During her tenure on the Supreme Court, O'Connor had the opportunity to rule on many significant cases. One of her first and more notable was *Mississippi University for Women v. Hogan* in 1982. She wrote the opinion for the court, explaining that it was unconstitutional for the all-women's school to refuse to admit men. Ten years later, she ruled in support of abortion rights in *Planned Parenthood v. Casey*. She also helped decide whether Florida's manual recount of presidential

FERRARO RUNS FOR VICE PRESIDENT

Geraldine Ferraro was the vice presidential running mate of Democratic candidate Walter Mondale in the 1984 presidential election. Ferraro was a US congresswoman from Queens, New York, where she was an assistant to the district attorney. She had a comfortable, down-to-earth personality and speaking style that resonated with men and women alike. Ferraro was also the first vice presidential candidate ever to speak about women's rights issues as a woman. Though she and Mondale did not win the 1984 election, Ferraro continued her political work, serving on the UN Commission on Human Rights between 1993 and 1996.

voting ballots in the 2000 election was constitutional. The landmark case, *Bush v. Gore*, was decided by a 5–4 vote, with O'Connor voting that the recount was unconstitutional.[7] When O'Connor retired from the Supreme Court in 2006, she left behind the only other female justice, Ruth Bader Ginsburg, who had been nominated in 1993. By 2010, two more women—Elena Kagan and Sonia Sotomayor—had joined the bench, bringing the total number of women who have ever served on the Supreme Court to four.

LaDuke Speaks for the Earth and Indigenous Women

When Mankiller became principal chief of the Cherokee Nation in Oklahoma, Winona LaDuke was hard at work on the White Earth

After her first speech in front of the UN in 1977, LaDuke spent her life as an activist.

Ojibwe Reservation in Minnesota advocating for the rights of native women and the right of tribes to manage tribal lands and address climate change issues.

In 1977, 18-year-old LaDuke spoke in front of the UN about the concerns and issues facing American Indians. After going to college, LaDuke returned to the White Earth Ojibwe Reservation to become a high school principal. She soon became involved in a dispute between the Ojibwe people and the federal government. The tribe hoped to recover lands guaranteed to the Ojibwe people in an 1867 treaty. LaDuke led the charge, but after four years of litigation, the Ojibwe's lawsuit was dismissed. Undeterred, LaDuke founded the Earth Land Recovery Project to continue the work of land recovery.

LaDuke's advocacy did not end in land recovery. In 1985, she cocreated the Indigenous Women's Network. The organization encourages native women to enter tribal government and make changes that improve the lives of women and families. She created another group in 1993 that supports native environmental groups. The Honor the Earth Fund

CHAVEZ TURNS FROM POLITICIAN TO PUNDIT

Republican Linda Chavez is a common sight on television news. The accomplished Latina politician, pundit, and writer served in the Reagan White House in the 1980s, first as the staff director of the US Commission on Civil Rights and later as the White House director of public liaison, the highest position held by a woman in Reagan's administration. In 1995, Chavez started the conservative think tank Center for Equal Opportunity, which opposes discrimination or preferences based on race in hiring and admission policies. She has written several books on political subjects and writes a weekly newspaper column.

supports campaigns to fight climate change and mining on tribal lands and improve tribal environmental policy.

LaDuke's hard work for native women, tribal rights, and the environment drew the attention of other political activists in the United States. *Time* magazine named her one of the most promising leaders under 40 years old in 1994, and in 1998, *Ms.* magazine named her Woman of the Year.[8] LaDuke also took the national stage when Ralph Nader asked her to be his running mate in the 1996 and 2000 presidential elections.

Whether running a nation, making history in the highest court in the land, or demanding rights for native women, women in the 1980s made great strides in government and politics. In the 1990s, a new class of women would carry on their work in the United States and around the world.

MIKULSKI SETS A RECORD

Barbara Mikulski was the longest-serving female member in the US Congress. She served five terms as US senator for the state of Maryland, 30 years total. Her long tenure makes her one of the more powerful senators. Before she was first elected in 1986, Mikulski served for ten years in the House of Representatives. She served on the Senate Appropriations Committee, which allocates federal money for government programs, for her entire career and chaired it between 2012 and 2016, the first woman to do so. Mikulski worked to improve access to education and for the rights of senior citizens, veterans, and women.

Bhutto became prime minister
of Pakistan in 1988.

CHAPTER FIVE

Women in the Political Mainstream

B y the end of the 1990s, although women were still outnumbered by men, it was no longer surprising to find them in leadership roles in government. From prime ministers and presidents in Pakistan and Burma to secretaries of state, attorneys, and justices in the United States, women were becoming part of the political mainstream.

Bhutto Fights Her Opposition

Benazir Bhutto spent most of the 1980s in exile or on house arrest. Her father had been the prime minister of Pakistan in the 1970s, but he was ousted and then executed by the military. Bhutto took up the leadership of her father's political party, the Pakistan People's Party (PPP), when he died, prompting the military to detain her. A decade of house arrest and exile came to a close when the country's military dictator died in a plane crash in 1988, and Bhutto led her party to victory in the national elections.

As prime minister, Bhutto pursued her ambitions of bringing democracy, personal freedom, and a more open society to Pakistan, despite objections from her political opponents. However, Bhutto found it difficult to make lasting change in the face of widespread poverty in Pakistan and entrenched corruption in the country's government. Bhutto herself could not escape corruption charges and was dismissed from the post of prime minister by Pakistan's president in 1990. Three years later, the PPP took back its majority in the national elections. As party leader, Bhutto was reappointed prime minister. Her second term lasted three years, when she was once again charged with corruption, including accepting bribes from a gold dealer, and dismissed in 1996.

After her dismissal, Bhutto went into self-imposed exile in the United Kingdom and the United Arab Emirates. Over the next few years, she battled the corruption charges from exile, and the courts overturned them in 2001. But the military, which had taken control of the government in 1999, did not recognize the reversal, so Bhutto remained in exile. She remained there until 2007, when the military government finally pardoned her from the corruption charges of the late 1990s. She returned to Pakistan in October 2007, surviving a suicide attack during celebrations in her honor. In December 2007, Bhutto was assassinated in another suicide attack while on the campaign trail.

Aung San Suu Kyi Fights for Democracy

Similar to Bhutto, Aung San Suu Kyi was the daughter of a prominent politician. Suu Kyi's father led the Burmese liberation movement in the 1940s. A military junta led the country between 1962 and 2011. It oppressed the civil rights of the Burmese people. In 1988, Suu Kyi began actively opposing the military government. She cofounded the National League for Democracy (NLD) political party in September 1988 to advocate for change through nonviolent protests. But when she and other protesters spoke out against the regime, they were met with violence. Thousands of protesters lost their lives. Through it all, Suu Kyi petitioned the government to allow democratic elections so Burmese citizens of all ethnicities would be represented in government.

Suu Kyi speaks in front of the UN in Geneva, Switzerland, in 2012.

Albright pushed Clinton to authorize air strikes to help Kosovo defend itself. But the Clinton administration dragged its feet on using force in Kosovo until January 15, 1999. That day, Serbian troops massacred dozens of Albanians in the village of Racak. The troops rounded up approximately 40 people, led them down to a gully, and shot them.[1] The massacre caused international outrage, and Clinton finally took action. US troops and UN forces worked together on the ground while diplomats, including Albright, led talks that resulted in peace.

After Clinton left office, Albright founded a consulting firm. In an interview about her time as secretary of state, Albright expressed pride for her work in Kosovo and other conflicts. "I went through some tough times," she said. "But I think that we would have been judged very, very harshly had we not stepped up to this."[2]

Reno Makes Tough Decisions

Janet Reno became the United States' first female attorney general in 1993 and stepped into some of the country's most infamous and controversial trials. Despite being appointed by President Clinton, Reno did not feel an obligation to act in his best interests. Instead, she considered the facts and circumstances of each case to decide its merits. By the end of her tenure in 2001, Reno was considered one of the most independent attorneys general in the history of the office.

After her appointment, Reno immediately stepped into one of the most controversial events in recent US history. On February 28, 1993, 12 days before Reno was sworn in as attorney general, the government attempted to serve search and arrest warrants at the compound of the Branch Davidians,

Madeleine Albright

When Albright became secretary of state, she already had a decades-long political career behind her. Her father was a diplomat from Czechoslovakia, where Albright was born. Her family fled the country when the Nazis invaded it in 1939. Her family returned briefly after World War II but found living in a now communist country difficult. They permanently moved to the United States in 1948.

Albright earned her PhD from Columbia University in New York. While in school, she worked on the 1972 presidential campaign of Senator Edmund Muskie. She joined the Jimmy Carter administration in 1976 as the assistant to the president's national security adviser. When Republican Ronald Reagan took office in 1981, Albright worked for several nonprofits and taught at Georgetown University in Washington, DC. She became the US ambassador to the United Nations in 1993 and secretary of state four years later.

(1937–)

Reno's expression of deep regret after the Branch Davidian incident helped her maintain good public opinion.

a radical Christian sect located in Waco, Texas, that law enforcement considered a cult. Officials believed the group was stockpiling weapons for an attack on its neighbors.

As agents approached the front door of the compound, shots rang out. Four agents were killed and 16 were wounded.[3] The deaths began a two-month standoff between the Branch Davidians and the US government.[4] After months of discussions with Federal Bureau of Investigation (FBI) officials and President Clinton, Reno decided to move ahead with a plan to conduct a raid with tear gas to force the Branch Davidians out and into custody. But the raid did not go as planned. As the FBI used large armored vehicles to launch tear gas into the compound, the property caught fire. Some Branch Davidians were able to escape, but more than 80 died.[5]

After the failed raid, the government launched an investigation into what went wrong. People disagreed whether the Branch Davidians started the fires or if the fires were caused by the tear gas. Reno testified that she authorized the use of tear gas because it seemed there was no other way to resolve the stalemate. She drew criticism for this decision and the decision to storm the compound in the first place. Reno accepted full responsibility for the raid and the lives lost.

Two years later, in 1995, Timothy McVeigh was charged and convicted of bombing the Alfred P. Murrah Federal Building in Oklahoma City, Oklahoma. The bombing killed 168 people.[6] Though personally against the death penalty, Reno authorized the government to seek it against Timothy McVeigh for his heinous act. She made the same decision two years later in the trial of Theodore Kaczynski. Kaczynski was charged and convicted of murdering three people and injuring 29 with bombs he sent through the mail.[7] While criticized for her actions in Waco, Reno was praised for the way she handled the trials of two notorious criminals.

Ginsburg Breaks Gender Barriers

A few months after the botched raid on Waco, Ruth Bader Ginsburg was sworn in as the second female Supreme Court justice. She had excelled in law school but discovered that no law firm would hire her on account of her gender. She attended Harvard Law School and then transferred to Columbia, where she graduated first in her class. Despite her stellar academic record, none of the 12 law firms she applied to would hire her.[8]

Prior to becoming a justice, Ginsburg
served on the US Court of Appeals in
Washington, DC.

In the 1960s and 1970s, Ginsburg taught law and volunteered her expertise with the American Civil Liberties Union (ACLU). Women's rights became a passion for Ginsburg. She cofounded the *Women's Rights Law Reporter*, which focused on women's rights and the law, and the ACLU's Women's Rights Project. As an attorney for the Women's Rights Project, Ginsburg argued several cases in front of the Supreme Court.

Ginsburg is an outspoken Supreme Court justice, even when she is the only one dissenting from the court's opinion. Her passion for women's rights extends to her work on the Supreme Court, where she has written court opinions for cases about workers' rights, gender equality, and civil liberties.

Women in government in the 1990s faced controversy, complex issues, and sometimes violent opposition. Building on the successes of female political leaders of earlier decades, women in the 1990s helped pave the way for younger women to take charge as a new millennium dawned in 2000.

REED V. REED

In 1971, the Supreme Court unanimously struck down a discriminatory law in Idaho that required state courts to favor men over women when deciding who could execute a will. The law had been in place since 1864 and was confirmed in a court challenge by Sally Reed in 1970. The Idaho State Supreme Court ruled that "men are better qualified to act as [administrators] than are women" and upheld the law.[9] Reed took her case to the Supreme Court, where Ginsburg helped plead her case. Ginsburg and her team argued Idaho's law violated the Fourteenth Amendment's Equal Protection Clause, which prohibits laws from making arbitrary preferences between genders and ethnicity. All of the justices of the Supreme Court agreed, and Idaho's law was struck down.

Merkel, *left*, and Sigurdardottir, *right*, shake hands after a joint meeting in 2011.

CHAPTER SIX

New Millennium, New Milestones

W hen the new millennium dawned in 2000, women across the world continued to break barriers and reach new milestones in the history of women in government. Several became heads of state in Europe, and two intrepid women helped bring peace and stability to Liberia. One woman became the first African-American female US secretary of state, and another the first female Speaker of the House.

Merkel, Tymoshenko, and Sigurdardottir Run Europe

Current longest-serving European head of government Angela Merkel is also Germany's first female chancellor. *Forbes* magazine has named her the most powerful woman in the world since she took office in 2005.[1] Merkel's political career started in 1989, when she became involved in the democracy movement in East Germany. Once East and West Germany were unified in

1990, Merkel joined the Christian Democratic Union political party, rising through the ranks over the next decade until she became the leader of the party in 2000. Five years later, she became chancellor of Germany.

As chancellor, Merkel has led Germany and the European Union (EU) through a debt crisis that began in 2007. She encouraged EU countries to pass austerity laws raising taxes and cutting spending rather than seek loans from countries with stronger economies, such as Germany. Her firmness during this time was not popular among struggling nations but garnered the support of many of her fellow Germans. In 2013, she helped negotiate an agreement between nations requiring countries to balance their national budgets.

Merkel has made Germany more active in foreign conflicts. She encouraged a diplomatic solution when Russia invaded the Crimean peninsula of Ukraine in 2014. Then Germany provided war supplies to forces fighting the radical group the Islamic State in Syria (ISIS). In the summer of 2015, she announced Germany would take in hundreds of thousands of Syrian refugees, a controversial decision as other European countries closed their borders to refugees.

Yulia Tymoshenko started her first term as Ukraine's prime minister the same year Merkel began her first term as chancellor. Tymoshenko entered politics in 1996 after a career in business. During her career in parliament, Tymoshenko became deputy prime minister for fuel and energy and generally supported energy policy that strengthened Ukraine's relationship with Russia. In 2001, she was dismissed from her post and convicted of corruption charges, which she claimed were politically motivated. The charges were later dropped, and she went on to lead the opposition to the current

Angela Merkel

Angela Merkel was raised in East Germany, which had become independent of West Germany after World War II. East Germany was under the influence of the communist Soviet Union, while the United States and its allies influenced West Germany. After earning a PhD in physics at the University of Leipzig, Merkel moved to East Berlin and became involved in a movement to promote democracy in East Germany.

East and West Germany reunified in 1990 after the fall of the Soviet Union, and Merkel entered the political scene. She served in Parliament first as the minister of women and youth and later as the minister of environment, conservation, and reactor safety. In 1999, Merkel criticized then-chancellor Helmut Kohl over a financial scandal that rocked his administration. Her popularity grew, and in 2000 she became leader of the Christian Democratic Union. After a failed bid in 2002, she became chancellor in 2005.

(1954–)

president, Viktor Yanukovych. Evidence of electoral fraud was uncovered, and Yanukovych was kicked out of office. Tymoshenko's ally Viktor Yushchenko became president—the head of the nation—and she became prime minister—the head of the government—in 2005. But within a year, Tymoshenko was dismissed from office.

However, Tymoshenko became prime minister once more in the 2007 elections on the promise of giving more power to the parliament. She fought to make Ukraine more democratic and became a leader in the prodemocracy and pro-Western Orange Revolution of 2004 and 2005. When she refused to recognize Yanukovych's victory in the 2010 presidential elections, she was promptly dismissed.

Between 2009 and 2011, Tymoshenko was convicted of abuse of power, tax evasion, and embezzlement while she was prime minister. Largely considered politically motivated, these convictions were overturned in 2014 and she was released from prison.

While Tymoshenko was battling abuse of power charges, Johanna Sigurdardottir was sworn in as Iceland's first female prime minister. She also became the first openly gay head of government in the world. She first became active in government in 1978 after a decade of advocating for workers' rights. As a parliamentarian, she fought to improve Iceland's welfare system and served as the minister of social affairs twice: once in the 1980s and again two years before she became prime minister. Her work for the disadvantaged earned her the nickname Saint Johanna.

In 2009, the conservative prime minister of Iceland resigned and Sigurdardottir became prime minister. As in the rest of Europe, Iceland was in the middle of an economic crisis. Sigurdardottir replaced the board members of the country's central bank, who failed to prevent the collapse of

Tymoshenko ran for
president once more in 2014
but lost to Petro Poroshenko.

Iceland's banks. Her government investigated the actions of the country's most powerful bankers and sent four of them to prison for fraud. Despite her government's tough stance against Iceland's bankers, she lost her seat as prime minister in 2013.

Gbowee Ends a War

While Merkel, Tymoshenko, and Sigurdardottir made strides in Europe, Leymah Gbowee was working to end a 14-year-long civil war in Liberia. The social worker and peace activist brought Christian and Muslim women together to take action for peace. She believed it was the responsibility of Liberia's women to secure peace for the next generation.

Gbowee was just 17 when Liberia's civil war broke out. She worked as a trauma counselor with children who had been forced to join the military and fight. Recruiting women from the Christian and Muslim faiths, Gbowee founded the Women of Liberia Mass Action for Peace organization. The group led protests to force Liberia's president, Charles Taylor, to start peace talks. Once negotiations began, the group encircled the meeting hall and refused to let the negotiators leave until they reached a peace agreement. Taylor resigned a few weeks later and a transitional government was put in place, led by future president Ellen Johnson Sirleaf.

Once she had helped bring an end to civil war, Gbowee continued her peace work. She was asked to speak at several UN Commission on the Status of Women conferences and in 2006 cofounded the Women Peace and Security Network Africa organization. The group works to get more African women to participate in government and lead peace-building efforts. In 2012, Gbowee expanded

Gbowee won the Nobel Peace Prize in 2011 for her work.

this work by founding the Gbowee Peace Foundation Africa to give girls and women more educational opportunities and leadership training.

Sirleaf Rebuilds Liberia

Gbowee's peacemaking work helped pave the way for Ellen

LIBERIA'S CIVIL WAR

Between 1989 and 2003, Liberia suffered through a violent civil war. Nearly 150,000 people died, mostly civilians.[2] The first phase of the war lasted between 1989 and 1997. Law and order gave way to violence, and the international community spent years trying to facilitate a peace agreement between the government and Taylor's opposition group National Patriotic Front of Liberia. Liberia held elections in 1997, and Taylor became president. After a few years of relative peace, violence again broke out in July 2003. Under pressure from Gbowee and other Liberian peace advocates, the fighting finally ended in peace talks and Taylor's resignation in August 2003.

Johnson Sirleaf to become Liberia's first female president and the first female president ever elected in Africa. She served in the federal government in the 1970s and 1980s as a minister of finance, but she was imprisoned in 1985 by military dictator Samuel Doe for criticizing his oppressive government. After a short time in prison, she was allowed to complete the rest of her sentence in exile in the United States and Kenya. During that time, Liberia's second civil war broke out.

Sirleaf put her time in exile to good use. She served in the UN Development Project for Africa and became the group's first female leader. In 1997, she returned to Liberia to run for president against incumbent Taylor. She came in second and had to flee the country again when he charged her with treason. Sirleaf led the Governance Reform Commission of the transitional government that replaced Taylor in 2003, during which time she gave more oversight power to the legislature and made anticorruption reforms.

Sirleaf ran for president in the November 2005 elections and won. As president, she improved the country's national security and expanded the country's infrastructure, building 800 miles (1,290 km) of roads.[3] The country's economy expanded greatly as Sirleaf opened the nation to foreign investment in mining, agriculture, and oil development. Between 2006 and 2011, Liberia's budget increased from $80 million to $500 million.[4] In 2011, Sirleaf won the Nobel Peace Prize for her peacemaking work.

Rice Advises Two Presidents

While Gbowee and Sirleaf were making peace in Liberia, Condoleezza Rice became the first female African-American secretary of state in the United States. Rice had already served more than six years collectively in the White House, first as President George H. W. Bush's expert on Soviet affairs on the National Security Council and later as President George W. Bush's national security adviser, the first woman to hold that position. George W. Bush appointed her secretary of state in 2005.

As secretary of state, Rice sent US diplomats to troubled regions across the world. These diplomats worked to effect change in areas rife with problems such as disease, drugs, and human trafficking. She also stood firm in negotiating sanctions against Iran to prevent the nation from acquiring a nuclear weapon. She helped find a solution to the chronic tension between Israel and Hezbollah, an Islamist political and military group. One of her landmark accomplishments was a trade deal with India that allowed the United States and India to trade nuclear material used in civil projects, such as power plants. Rice went on to start a consulting firm to help senior executives of large corporations trade goods and services overseas.

"THIS IS CONDOLEEZZA RICE"

Condoleezza Rice was 35 years old when she became President George H. W. Bush's expert on Soviet and Eastern Europe Affairs in 1989. Despite her age, Rice had a deep understanding of the Soviet political system. President Bush introduced Rice to Soviet president Mikhail Gorbachev in 1989. "This is Condoleezza Rice," he said. "She tells me everything I know about the Soviet Union." Gorbachev replied, "I hope she knows a lot."[5] At first, the older, male Soviet diplomats were skeptical of Rice's ability to be tough in negotiations regarding the military and politics. But Rice proved her knowledge and her diplomacy skills, and the skepticism soon dissipated.

Rice left the office of secretary of state
when President Obama was sworn in.

Pelosi Fights for the Middle Class

In 2007, two years into Rice's tenure as secretary of state, US representative Nancy Pelosi was sworn in as the first female Speaker of the House. During her five-year tenure, the House of Representatives passed legislation that increased the minimum wage, supported clean energy development, and raised fuel efficiency standards. It also expanded educational opportunities for veterans of the Iraq and Afghanistan wars.

The two largest issues the House tackled while Pelosi was Speaker were the American Recovery and Reinvestment Act and the Affordable Care Act. The American Recovery and Reinvestment Act was passed to alleviate the economic crisis that occurred in the fall of 2008. It created job opportunities for Americans and cut taxes.

The Affordable Care Act expanded health-care access and gave Americans more choice in health insurance. It also abolished lifetime money limits on health care.

Pelosi's Democratic political party lost its majority in the House during the 2010 elections, and she handed the gavel to new Speaker John Boehner in 2011. She became the leader of the minority party in the House and continued to focus her efforts on providing more opportunities for the middle class and encouraging the United States to adopt cleaner energy resources.

The 2000s were a time of drastic political and social change, and women were often at the forefront. They continued to tackle some of the world's most pressing issues after 2010. Two would even run for the highest and most powerful political office in the United States.

Pelosi's leadership as Speaker helped create one of the most productive Congresses in history.

Park was elected president of South Korea on the promise to strengthen national security and the economy.

CHAPTER SEVEN

Facing Challenges

In the 2010s, women continued to take on leadership roles in governments across the globe. While some countries embraced the reality or possibility of a female head of government, others continued to oppress the rights of women and other citizens. Through the triumphs and the challenges, women continued to speak up and lead.

Park Geun-Hye Breaks Barriers in South Korea

Park Geun-Hye's election as president of South Korea in 2013 was simultaneously celebrated and controversial. She became the first female president in the country with the worst gender inequality in the developed world, but her achievement was overshadowed by her family's controversial past.

Park's father was former South Korean president Park Chung-Hee, who had overthrown the previous administration and seized power in 1963. Geun-Hye had served as his First Lady for a few years after her mother died. When Chung-Hee was assassinated in 1979, Geun-Hye continued her career in politics. In 1998, she was elected to the National Assembly as a member of the conservative Grand National Party and served as party chairperson between 2004 and 2006. She was reelected four times before 2012.

In 2012, Park ran for president against her more progressive opponent, who was a human rights attorney her father had imprisoned during his rule. Park's family history has been a persistent issue in her political life. While some respected Park Chung-Hee as the man who saved South Korea's economy, others vilified him as a ruthless dictator. In her presidential campaign, Park did not shy away from speaking about her father's controversial regime. She publicly apologized for his brutality while adopting his slogan "Let's live well" as her own.[1]

As president, she faced the immediate challenge of stabilizing South Korea's relationship with its communist and nuclear-armed neighbor North Korea, ruled by an ironhanded dictator. Soon after Park was sworn in in early 2013, the relationship deteriorated to the point that a shared industrial zone was closed for the first time. After a few months of uncertainty, the relationship restabilized, and talks soon began again to allow family visits across the border. South Korea's relationships with other neighbors were rosier. Park signed an environmental cooperation treaty with China and Japan and a trade agreement with Canada. Despite these triumphs, Park lost popularity in 2014 and 2015 due to stagnant

Clooney has worked on several high-profile cases throughout her career.

consumer spending and decreased wages. She had not yet made good on her promise to improve the economy.

Clooney Defends the Vulnerable

Amal Alamuddin Clooney was 27 years old when she joined the UN tribunal team that prosecuted the people who assassinated Lebanese prime minister Rafic Hariri. Born in Lebanon herself, Clooney's family fled Lebanon during its civil war that began in the 1970s and was still raging in 1980. Her family settled in England, where Clooney excelled in law school and started building her reputation as one of the world's top human rights and international law attorneys.

Since her work on the prosecution in the Hariri case, Clooney has worked on dozens of high-profile human rights and international law cases. She argues cases in front of the International Criminal Court, the International Court of Justice, and the European Court of Human Rights. She advises governments and other groups on sexual violence during conflict, explaining how to find justice for sexual violence victims and how sexual violence is used as a weapon of war. She also advises governments and groups on the legal implications of using drones, including their impact on human rights.

Clooney has represented several high-profile international figures. She was part of Yulia Tymoshenko's legal team in Tymoshenko's challenge of her conviction and imprisonment in 2011. And she represented WikiLeaks founder Julian Assange during his legal proceedings over alleged

INTERNATIONAL CRIMINAL COURT

When Amal Clooney argues cases at the International Criminal Court (ICC), they involve only the most serious international crimes. Located in the Netherlands, the ICC is a court of last resort, only hearing cases where the defendant is accused of the worst crimes: genocide, war crimes, and crimes against humanity. In the fall of 2015, the ICC was hearing cases for crimes committed in Kenya, Libya, the Central African Republic, the Democratic Republic of Congo, and five other nations. It was considering taking cases for crimes committed in nine others.[2]

sexual assault in Sweden. Despite her efforts to fight Assange's extradition from the United Kingdom to Sweden, the UK Supreme Court approved the extradition. She was appointed former UN Secretary-General Kofi Annan's senior adviser when he traveled to Syria to investigate human rights abuses there at the outbreak of its civil war in 2012.

Pussy Riot Stands Up to Censorship

In February 2012, the Russian feminist punk rock group Pussy Riot took the stage at the orthodox cathedral in Moscow, Russia. They were protesting the conservative and sometimes oppressive government in Russia and its close ties to the conservative orthodox church. "Birth-giver of God, drive away Putin!" the band sang, demanding an end to Russian president Vladimir Putin's regime.[3] Three members of Pussy Riot were arrested that night on charges of disruptive behavior. All three members were sentenced in August 2012 to two years in prison. Yekaterina Samutsevich won an appeal of her sentence and was released in October 2012.

The arrest and conviction of the Pussy Riot band members drew widespread criticism from many of Russia's

MUSIC AS POLITICAL PROTEST

Pussy Riot is not the first band to use music to make a political protest. Protest music was especially popular in the United States after World War II. Musicians expressed their opposition to the government's treatment of African Americans during the civil rights movement and also their opposition to the Vietnam War. "We Shall Overcome" was the anthem of the civil rights movement in the 1950s and 1960s. Protesters sang it while marching, in the face of police violence, and in jail cells.

international partners, including the United States. In December 2013, Maria Alyokhina and Nadezhda Tolokonnikova were released from prison shortly before the 2014 Winter Games in Sochi, Russia, along with 25,000 other political prisoners.[4] As soon as they were released, the musicians condemned their release as a political stunt. They pledged to take up prison reform as their new political cause.

Alyokhina and Tolokonnikova became sought-after speakers in the international community and visited New York City's Rikers Island prison in 2014. In June 2015, Tolokonnikova was arrested in Moscow while protesting Putin and Russia's oppressive treatment of female inmates. She was wearing the same uniform she wore while in prison a few years before.

Yellen Takes the Helm of the Fed

When Janet Yellen became the first female chairperson of the Board of Governors of the Federal Reserve System, also called the Fed, the US central bank was still trying to find its footing and foster growth in the US economy after the 2008 recession. Her predecessor, Ben Bernanke, had helped avert disaster in the wake of the recession but failed to anticipate and prevent it. Bernanke resigned as chairman in 2013.

Yellen was no stranger to the Fed and the central banking system. An economics professor at the University of California–Berkeley, Yellen took a position on the Board of Governors in 1994. She left the board in 1997 to lead two economic policy organizations. She held these positions for two years before returning to teaching in 1999.

President Obama appointed Yellen as Bernanke's replacement.

Yellen was pulled out of teaching once again in 2004 to become the president of the Federal Reserve branch in San Francisco, a position she held for six years before becoming the vice chair of the Board of Governors. In 2013, President Obama nominated her as the next chairperson of the Fed.

In her first year, Yellen reduced the unemployment rate by more than 1 percent and inflation was below target, despite continued worry of some economists.[5] She allows data, rather than politics or intuition, to guide her economic policy decisions. A future challenge for Yellen will be the decision to finally raise interest rates, which the Fed has deliberately kept low since 2008 for fear of triggering another crisis.

Fiorina and Clinton Run for President

The 2016 US election cycle included two women. Former chief executive officer (CEO) Carly Fiorina ran for the Republican ticket, and former First Lady, senator, and secretary of state Hillary Clinton ran as a Democrat. It was the first time two women had been serious contenders for US president.

Republican Carly Fiorina has a strong business background. She was the first woman to lead a company large enough to be listed on the Dow Jones Industrial Average, an average of the price of the stock of 30 industrial companies. She became CEO of the computer company Hewlett-Packard (HP) in 1999. The company was struggling to remain profitable, and Fiorina was tasked with righting the ship. In six years, Fiorina claimed to have quadrupled HP's growth rate and doubled its revenues. It went from being the twenty-eighth-largest company in the United States to eleventh.[6] Despite these accomplishments, however, Fiorina failed to make a merger with Compaq Computer Corporation meet profit expectations.

After leaving HP, Fiorina began a career in politics. She became a commentator on Fox News and a consultant to Senator John McCain's 2008 presidential campaign. She led the American Conservative Union Foundation, which hosts a conference for conservative politicians every year. She unsuccessfully ran against Barbara Boxer, a Democrat, in the 2009 California Senate race. She announced she was running for president in May 2015. She had a strong showing in the September 2015 debate

Fiorina was forced to resign from HP in 2005, leading to her political career.

between Republican candidates, but her popularity decreased in the polls and she ended her bid in February 2016.

Democrat Hillary Clinton is no stranger to politics. As a young attorney in 1974, Clinton worked on the inquiry into President Richard Nixon's involvement in a wiretapping scandal called Watergate. She moved to Little Rock, Arkansas, and joined a law firm there in 1975. That same year, she married Bill

Clinton, who became the governor of Arkansas in 1978. As First Lady of Arkansas, Clinton continued her career as an attorney, a rare move for a First Lady in the late 1970s. She also used the power of her office to advocate for programs that helped women and children.

Clinton was the first First Lady to have a significant career of her own and to be active in her husband's presidential campaign. This raised the eyebrows of the more conservative members of Congress, who claimed Clinton was trying to force her own agenda on the White House after Bill won the presidency in 1992. These criticisms grew louder when Clinton asked for her own office in the West Wing of the White House. As First Lady, Clinton continued to advocate for women and children. President Clinton appointed her to lead the Task Force on National Health Care.

In 2000, Clinton became the first First Lady to be elected to the US Senate. She continued to advocate for health-care reform in the Senate and also sat on the Committee for Armed Service. She was reelected in 2006 and announced her candidacy for president in 2008. After a hard-fought battle for the nomination, Clinton conceded to Senator Barack Obama, who was elected president in November 2008. Obama called Clinton to a secret meeting in 2008, where he asked her to become his secretary of state.

Clinton served as secretary of state between 2009 and 2013. She worked to improve US relationships with countries around the world. In the Middle East, she helped negotiate a cease-fire between Israel and Hamas and fought for economic sanctions against Iran. She also focused on strengthening trade relationships in Asia and advocated for more women's involvement in politics worldwide. She strongly supported President Obama's decision to attack Osama bin

Laden's compound, an act that garnered bipartisan support after the secret mission was declared a success. But Clinton's controversial handling of the United States' involvement in the overthrow of Libyan dictator Muammar al-Qaddafi drew criticism, especially in failing to anticipate the attack on the US embassy in Benghazi that left an ambassador and three other Americans dead.[7]

Her actions in Benghazi became the focus of her opposition when she declared her campaign for president in 2015. She endured an 11-hour investigation on the subject led by House Republicans.[8] In June 2016, Clinton won the Democratic presidential nomination. She was the first woman to become the presidential nominee of any major US political party.

Clinton's platform included gun violence prevention, immigration reform, and health care, among other important issues.

The Malala Fund works all over the developing world.

CHAPTER EIGHT

Breaking Glass Ceilings

A fter Malala accepted her Nobel Peace Prize in 2014, she started the Malala Fund to help empower girls and expand access to education for girls in developing countries. Malala hopes to devote her life to fighting for girls' education, a cause that many women and organizations across the world also support.

A Trio of Organizations Help Girls Rise

The Malala Fund's goal is to make 12 complete years of education available to girls everywhere.[1] It brings girls together to share their experiences, overcome challenges, and advocate for themselves. The organization also funds groups that support girls' education and presses governments to change their laws and policies to make it easier for girls to get an education.

The Malala Fund pays for education for girls in refugee camps and rural Pakistan, Kenya, Nigeria, Lebanon, and Jordan. It organizes classes for girls in technology and life skills. It gets groups of teenage girls together for fellowship, to find solutions to challenges, and to gain confidence.

Similar to the Malala Fund, Girl Rising supports girls' education. Cofounder Holly Gordon has built a leadership team composed nearly entirely of women. Its primary goal is to make girls' education a priority in countries around the world. Its main tool to raise awareness is the documentary film *Girl Rising*. It provides schools with curriculum materials so the film can be used in the classroom. Girl Rising ENGAGE (Empowering Next Generations to Advance Girls' Education) works with the US Agency for International Development to expand education in India, the Democratic Republic of Congo, and West Africa.

Girls Inc. is a North American group that started at the turn of the 1900s in New England. Since then, it has supported programs that help girls become confident, strong, and smart. The organization funds programs that put together trained staff, volunteers, and mentors to help girls succeed. They may provide girls with science and math

THE GIRLS' BILL OF RIGHTS

There are six rights outlined in the Girls Inc. Girls' Bill of Rights.

- Girls have the right to be themselves and resist gender stereotypes.
- Girls have the right to express themselves with originality and enthusiasm.
- Girls have the right to take risks, to strive freely, and to take pride in success.
- Girls have the right to accept and appreciate their bodies.
- Girls have the right to have confidence in themselves and to be safe in the world.
- Girls have the right to prepare for interesting work and economic independence.

education, tools to prevent violence, and the skills to understand and interpret what happens in the media and the economy. Girls Inc. also pressures federal political leaders to pass legislation that supports girls.

UN Women Strives for Gender Equality

Expanding access to education is a powerful way to improve the quality of life for girls and can even lift families out of poverty. So can providing education for women and eliminating gender barriers in the economy, society, and politics. In July 2010, the UN created UN Women, an organization that organizes and oversees the UN's efforts to reduce gender inequality.

The UN believes gender equality is a basic human right. The group hopes to empower women and eliminate discrimination against girls and women. UN Women works with members of the UN to create policies that encourage countries to reduce discrimination against women and girls.

Women Continue to Fight for Political Power

Women in the United States were granted the right to vote in 1920, and by the time the Voting Rights Act of 1965 passed, all female US citizens were able to vote and participate in US politics. Nearly 100 years after Jeannette Rankin became the first female member of Congress, women continue to fight for equity in politics, the economy, and society. Of 535 members of Congress, 104 are women. There are 20 female senators out of 100 total in the legislative body, and in the House, 84 of 435 representatives are women. Only four women have ever served on the Supreme Court. By 2016,

Alaa Murabit

(1989–)

Women's rights activist Alaa Murabit was 21 years old when she founded her organization, the Voice of Libyan Women (VLW), in 2011. Her family had fled Libya for Canada in the 1980s, but Murabit returned there after graduating from high school at the age of 15. She quickly learned the freedoms she enjoyed as a teenager in Canada were not available to women and girls in Libya because of oppressive laws. The country's religious leaders justified many of these laws.

In 2015, Murabit sat on several UN groups, including the UN Women Global Advisory Board. She founded VLW to advocate against gender violence, train women to become civically active, and research how to best ensure women are safe and secure in their communities. Often this means challenging a community's accepted views and treatment of women. Yemen, Jordan, and Saudi Arabia have all asked for VLW's help in making their societies safer for women. The VLW's Noor Campaign fights misrepresentation of Islamic teachings that help countries and clerics justify discriminating against women. The group purchases ad space on billboards, television, and radio to shed light on what Islam teaches on how women should be treated.

no woman had ever served as president of the United States.[2]

Globally, 22 percent of the world's legislators are women. This number is double what it was in 1995.[3] In some countries, the road to elected office is long and difficult. In others, it is still a dream. Until August 2015, women in Saudi Arabia could neither vote nor run for political office. Saudi King Abdullah announced his intention to allow women to vote and run in local elections in 2011. Saudi Arabia is a monarchy, but local government officials are elected. In 2013, King Abdullah decreed that 20 percent of his advisory council would be women too.[4] These changes to Saudi Arabia's laws are a step in the right direction, but Saudi women still face many barriers to finding gender equality in politics. Saudi women, for example, are not allowed to drive. Though they have the right to vote, they may not be able to get themselves to the voting booths.

VOTER ID ACTS

In the 2010s, several states in the United States passed voter ID acts. Supporters of these laws believe that requiring voters to present identification when they vote will reduce voter fraud. But critics believe voter ID laws may make it more difficult for people to exercise their right to vote. Shortly after Tennessee passed its voter ID act, an elderly woman who had voted all her adult life was denied a photo ID card that would identify her at the polls. Though she presented her birth certificate, her voter ID card, a copy of her lease, and a rent receipt, the names on these documents did not match. Some of them had her maiden name, others her married one. This complication nearly exclusively affects women.

Helping Women and Girls Helps the World

Armed with a secondary education, a girl is six times less likely to marry before she turns 18. This means she is waiting to start her family, too, and will have fewer—but healthier—children. If all women in developing countries finished high school, the mortality rate for children under five years old would be cut nearly in half.[5] A girl who is given the opportunity to earn a secondary education will likely make more money and break her family's cycle of poverty.

Whether it is a woman registering to vote in Saudi Arabia or a girl of color completing high school and studying engineering in college, enfranchising and educating women and girls benefits individuals, their families, their communities, and society. But empowering women at the voting booth and in the classroom today would not be possible without the hard work of generations of women determined to give women political power and a political voice.

WHAT SAUDI WOMEN CANNOT DO

Though Saudi women can now vote and run in local elections, they still face widespread gender discrimination in Saudi culture, economic life, and politics. In addition to being banned from driving, women are not able to travel or go to school without male guardians. A woman must also have her husband's permission to open a bank account. Strict religious laws dictate what women can wear and forbid makeup that enhances a woman's natural beauty. Women cannot go swimming, try on clothes at a clothing store, or compete in sports.

Saudi Arabian women earned the right to vote in 2015. The country was one of the last to grant this privilege.

Timeline

1916
Jeannette Rankin becomes the first female member of the US Congress.

1946
Eleanor Roosevelt is appointed chair of the UN Commission on Human Rights.

1955
Rosa Parks refuses to give up her seat on a Montgomery, Alabama, city bus.

1967
Dolores Huerta and Cesar Chavez merge two farmworkers groups into the United Farm Workers Organizing Committee.

1969
Golda Meir becomes prime minister of Israel; Shirley Chisholm becomes the first female African American to enter the US Congress.

1971
Gloria Steinem and others found the National Women's Political Caucus.

1977
Wangari Maathai founds the Green Belt Movement in Kenya.

1979
Shirin Ebadi loses her position as chief justice in Iran's Islamic Revolution; Margaret Thatcher becomes the first female prime minister of the United Kingdom.

1981
Sandra Day O'Connor is appointed the first female justice of the US Supreme Court.

1985
Wilma Mankiller becomes principal chief of the Cherokee Nation.

1988

Benazir Bhutto becomes prime minister of Pakistan.

1991

Aung San Suu Kyi is awarded the Nobel Peace Prize.

1993

Winona LaDuke founds the Honor the Earth Fund;
Janet Reno is appointed US attorney general; Ruth
Bader Ginsburg is appointed to the US Supreme Court.

1997

Madeleine Albright is appointed US secretary of state.

2003

Shirin Ebadi is the first Muslim woman to win the
Nobel Peace Prize.

2004

Wangari Maathai is the first African woman to receive
the Nobel Peace Prize.

2005

Angela Merkel is elected chancellor of Germany; Yulia
Tymoshenko is elected prime minister of Ukraine;
Condoleezza Rice is appointed US secretary of state.

2007

Nancy Pelosi is sworn in as US Speaker of the House.

2009

Johanna Sigurdardottir is elected prime minister
of Iceland.

2013

Park Geun-Hye is elected the first female president of
South Korea.

2014

Malala Yousafzai is awarded the Nobel Peace Prize.

Essential Facts

KEY PLAYERS

- Indira Gandhi, first female prime minister of India

- Betty Friedan, author of *The Feminine Mystique*

- Shirley Chisholm, first African-American woman to serve in the US legislative branch

- Margaret Thatcher, prime minister of the United Kingdom

- Leymah Gbowee, political activist in Liberia

- Malala Yousafzai, girls' education activist in Pakistan

WOMEN AS POLITICIANS AND GOVERNMENT OFFICIALS

Women have not always had the opportunity to work in government and politics. In 2015, there were some countries around the world where women were still being granted the right to vote. US women earn 60 percent of undergraduate degrees and 60 percent of master's degrees in the United States. US women are 59 percent of the college-educated, entry-level US labor force. Yet, despite these numbers, few women hold leadership positions. However, between 1995 and 2005, the number of women in governments worldwide nearly doubled. As of August 2015, 13 women were heads of government and 12 were heads of state around the world.

IMPACT ON SOCIETY

When women participate in government, there is increased cooperation both within the government and between governments, better response to the needs of citizens, and increased peace between nations and social and ethnic groups.

QUOTE

"Equality of rights under the law shall not be denied or abridged by the United States or by any state on account of sex."

—*Equal Rights Amendment*

Glossary

APPEAL
To ask for a court decision to be overturned.

AUSTERITY
Reduced spending by governments to shrink debt levels.

BOYCOTT
To refuse to have dealings with, usually in order to express disapproval or to force acceptance of certain conditions.

CLERIC
A religious official.

DIPLOMACY
The skill of maintaining relationships between governments.

DISENFRANCHISE
To deprive a group of a legal right.

GENOCIDE
The deliberate mass murder of a group of people.

HAMAS
An Islamic political group in Palestine and the Middle East.

HEZBOLLAH
An Islamist militant group and political party in Lebanon.

INFLATION
An increase in the price of goods and services.

JUNTA
A group that controls a government after a revolution.

LITIGATION
Argument of a lawsuit.

MALNOURISHED
Poorly fed and lacking essential nutrients to thrive.

MILITANT
Aggressively supporting a cause.

NATIONALIST

Someone who supports his or her nation above all others.

PARLIAMENT

The supreme legislative body of a country.

PRIME MINISTER

The head of a government.

RATIFY

To formally approve or adopt an idea or document.

THEOCRACY

A country governed by religious leaders.

THINK TANK

A group that thinks up solutions to large social, political, and economic problems.

UNION

A formal organization of workers.

Additional Resources

SELECTED BIBLIOGRAPHY

Cullen-DuPont, Kathryn ed. *American Women Activists' Writings: An Anthology, 1637–2002*. New York: Cooper Square, 2002. Print.

Janda, Sarah Eppler. *Beloved Women: The Political Lives of LaDonna Harris and Wilma Mankiller*. DeKalb, IL: Northern Illinois UP, 2007. Print.

"Woman Suffrage Timeline." *National Women's History Museum*. National Women's History Museum, n.d. Web. 8 Jan. 2016.

Yousafzai, Malala. "Nobel Lecture." *Nobelprize.org*. Nobel Media AB, 10 Dec. 2014. Web. 8 Jan. 2016.

FURTHER READINGS

Cupp, Tonya Maddox. *Angela Merkel: First Woman Chancellor of Germany*. New York: Cavendish Square, 2015. Print.

Winslow, Barbara. *Shirley Chisholm: Catalyst for Change, 1926–2005*. Boulder, CO: Westview, 2014. Print.

Yousafzai, Malala. *I Am Malala: How One Girl Stood Up for Education and Changed the World*. New York: Little, Brown, 2014. Print.

WEBSITES

To learn more about Women's Lives in History, visit **booklinks.abdopublishing.com**. These links are routinely monitored and updated to provide the most current information available.

FOR MORE INFORMATION

For more information on this subject, contact or visit the following organizations:

United Nations Headquarters
405 East 42nd Street
New York, NY 10017
212-963-1234
www.un.org
Take a tour of UN headquarters and see where UN ambassadors meet. Tours are available in six languages.

US Capitol
East Capitol Street NE
Washington, DC 20004
202-226-8000
https://www.visitthecapitol.gov
Walk the halls and see US representatives and senators. Visit the offices of your state's congressional representatives.

The White House
1600 Pennsylvania Avenue NW
Washington, DC 20500
202-456-1111
https://www.whitehouse.gov
See inside the president's offices in the West Wing and other areas of the White House.

Source Notes

CHAPTER 1. BREAKING GROUND

1. Malala Yousafzai. "Nobel Lecture." *NobelPrize.org*. Nobel Media AB, 10 Dec. 2014. Web. 27 Jan. 2016.

2. "Nobel Prize Awarded Women." *NobelPrize.org*. Nobel Media AB, 2014. Web. 27 Jan. 2016.

3. Malala Yousafzai. "Nobel Lecture." *NobelPrize.org*. Nobel Media AB, 10 Dec. 2014. Web. 27 Jan. 2016.

4. "Biography of Susan B Anthony." *National Susan B. Anthony Museum & House*. Susan B. Anthony House, 2013. Web. 27 Jan. 2016.

5. "Woman Suffrage Timeline." *National Women's History Museum*. National Women's History Museum, n.d. Web. 27 Jan. 2016.

6. Associated Press. "Saudi Women Go to Polls in Landmark Election." *Guardian*. Guardian News, 12 Dec. 2015. Web. 27 Jan. 2016.

7. "The Nobel Peace Prize: Awarded to 129 Nobel Laureates since 1901." *NobelPrize.org*. Nobel Media AB, 2014. Web. 27 Jan. 2016.

CHAPTER 2. SETTING THE STAGE FOR CHANGE

1. Betty Friedan. *The Feminine Mystique*. New York: W. W. Norton, 1963. *National Humanities Center*. Web. 27 Jan. 2016.

2. Susan Seligson. "Friedan's *Feminine Mystique* Turns 50." *BU Today*. Boston University, 12 Feb. 2013. Web. 27 Jan. 2016.

3. Roberta W. Francis and Bettina Hager. "The Equal Rights Amendment." *ERA Task Force*. National Council of Women's Organizations, March 2013. Web. 27 Jan. 2016.

4. "The Story Behind the Bus." *Henry Ford*. Henry Ford, 2002. Web. 27 Jan. 2016.

5. Editors of Encyclopædia Britannica. "Apartheid." *Encyclopædia Britannica*. Encyclopædia Britannica, 3 June 2015. Web. 27 Jan. 2016.

6. "Delores Clara Fernandez Huerta (1930–)." *National Women's History Museum*. National Women's History Museum, n.d. Web. 27 Jan. 2016.

CHAPTER 3. MAKING WAVES IN COURT AND CONGRESS

1. "Chisholm, Shirley Anita." *History, Art & Archives*. Office of the Historian, n.d. Web. 27 Jan. 2016.

2. "National Women's Political Caucus." *Texas Law*. University of Texas at Austin, 2016. Web. 27 Jan. 2016.

3. Ibid.

4. "Women in State Legislatures for 2015." *National Conference of State Legislatures*. National Conference of State Legislatures, 4 Sept. 2015. Web. 27 Jan. 2016.

5. "Our History." *Congressional Black Caucus Foundation*. Congressional Black Caucus Foundation, 2016. Web. 27 Jan. 2016.

6. Tiffany E. Dalpe. "Sarah Weddington." *Encyclopædia Britannica*. Encyclopædia Britannica, 30 Oct. 2014. Web. 27 Jan. 2016.

7. Roberta W. Francis and Bettina Hager. "The Equal Rights Amendment." *ERA Task Force*. National Council of Women's Organizations, March 2013. Web. 27 Jan. 2016.

8. "Wangari Maathai—Facts." *NobelPrize.org*. Nobel Media AB, 2014. Web. 27 Jan. 2016.

9. "The Female Face of Farming." *Farming First*. Farming First, n.d. Web. 27 Jan. 2016.

10. Ibid.

11. "Shirin Ebadi—Iran, 2003." *Nobel Women's Initiative*. Nobel Women's Initiative, n.d. Web. 27 Jan. 2016.

CHAPTER 4. WOMEN RISING

1. Sam Howe Verhovek. "Wilma Mankiller, Cherokee Chief and First Woman to Lead Major Tribe, Is Dead at 64." *New York Times*. New York Times Company, 6 Apr. 2010. Web. 27 Jan. 2016.

2. "Trail of Tears." *National Park Service*. National Park Service, 15 Jan. 2016. Web. 27 Jan. 2016.

3. "The Trail of Tears." *Africans in America*. WGBH Educational Foundation, 1999. Web. 27 Jan. 2015.

4. Sam Howe Verhovek. "Wilma Mankiller, Cherokee Chief and First Woman to Lead Major Tribe, Is Dead at 64." *New York Times*. New York Times Company, 6 Apr. 2010. Web. 27 Jan. 2016.

5. "Sandra Day O'Connor." *Makers*. Makers, 2016. Web. 27 Jan. 2016.

Source Notes Continued

6. "Sandra Day O'Connor Biography." *Sandra Day O'Connor Institute.* Sandra Day O'Connor, 2015. Web. 27 Jan. 2016.

7. "Bush v. Gore." *Oyez.* Chicago-Kent College of Law at Illinois Tech, n.d. Web. 27 Jan. 2016.

8. "Winona LaDuke." *National Women's Hall of Fame.* National Women's Hall of Fame, 2016. Web. 27 Jan. 2016.

CHAPTER 5. WOMEN IN THE POLITICAL MAINSTREAM

1. Jon Silverman. "Racak Massacre Haunts Milosevic Trial." *BBC News.* BBC, 14 Feb. 2002. Web. 27 Jan. 2016.

2. "Madeleine Albright." *Frontline.* WGBH Educational Foundation, 2014. Web. 27 Jan. 2016.

3. "Chronology of the Siege" *Frontline.* WGBH Educational Foundation, 2014. Web. 27 Jan. 2016.

4. Ibid.

5. "Frequently Asked Questions About Waco." *Frontline.* WGBH Educational Foundation, 2014. Web. 27 Jan. 2016.

6. John F. Fox Jr. "Impact of the Oklahoma City Bombing 20 Years Later." *Newseum.* Newseum, 17 Apr. 2015. Web. 27 Jan. 2016.

7. Greg Lefevre. "Kaczynski Pleads Guilty, Avoids Death Sentence." *CNN.com.* Cable News Network, 22 Jan. 1998. Web. 27 Jan. 2016.

8. "Ruth Bader Ginsburg." *Makers.* Makers, 2016. Web. 27 Jan. 2016.

9. "Breaking New Ground: *Reed v. Reed.*" *Supreme Court Historical Society.* Supreme Court Historical Society, n.d. Web. 27 Jan. 2016.

CHAPTER 6. NEW MILLENNIUM, NEW MILESTONES

1. "#2 Angela Merkel." *Forbes.* Forbes.com, 2016. Web. 27 Jan. 2016.

2. "UNMIL Background." *United Nations Mission in Liberia.* United Nations, n.d. Web. 27 Jan. 2016.

3. "Biographical Brief of Ellen Johnson Sirleaf." *Executive Mansion.* Executive Mansion, n.d. Web. 27 Jan. 2016.

4. Ibid.

5. "Condoleezza Rice." *Makers.* Makers, 2016. Web. 27 Jan. 2016.

CHAPTER 7. FACING CHALLENGES

1. André Munro. "Park Geun-Hye." *Encyclopædia Britannica*. Encyclopædia Britannica, 30 Oct. 2014. Web. 27 Jan. 2016.

2. "Frequently Asked Questions." *International Criminal Court*. International Criminal Court, n.d. Web. 27 Jan. 2016.

3. Melena Ryzik. "Founding Member of Pussy Riot Detained in Moscow." *New York Times*. New York Times Company, 12 June 2015. Web. 27 Jan. 2016.

4. Olga L. Medvedkov. "Russia." *Encyclopædia Britannica*. Encyclopædia Britannica, 10 Oct. 2015. Web. 27 Jan. 2016.

5. Joe Weisenthal. "Janet Yellen Just Completed a Great First Year. Year Two Will Be Harder." *Bloomberg Business*. Bloomberg, 3 Feb. 2015. Web. 27 Jan. 2016.

6. Alan Stewart. "Carly Fiorina." *Encyclopædia Britannica*. Encyclopædia Britannica, 11 Aug. 2015. Web. 27 Jan. 2016.

7. Walter Russell Mead. "Was Hillary Clinton a Good Secretary of State?" *Washington Post*. Washington Post, 30 May 2014. Web. 27 Jan. 2016.

8. Sam Frizell. "How Hillary Clinton Won the Benghazi Hearing." *TIME*. Time, 23 Oct. 2015. Web. 27 Jan. 2016.

CHAPTER 8. BREAKING GLASS CEILINGS

1. "About the Malala Fund." *Malala Fund*. Malala Fund, n.d. Web. 27 Jan. 2016.

2. Heather Jones and Charlotte Alter. "This Graphic Shows Why We Still Need Women's Equality Day." *TIME*. Time, 26 Aug. 2015. Web. 27 Jan. 2016.

3. Eli Watkins. "Saudi Suffragettes: Women Register to Vote for the First Time in Saudi Arabia." *CNN*. Cable New Network, 23 Aug. 2015. Web. 27 Jan. 2016.

4. Ibid.

5. "Girls' Education." *Malala Fund*. Malala Fund, n.d. Web. 27 Jan. 2016.

Index

About the Author

Amanda Lanser is a freelance writer who lives in Minneapolis, Minnesota. She is the author of books on a variety of topics from President Woodrow Wilson and World War I to boa constrictors and Ötzi the Iceman. She enjoys writing for kids of all ages.